This Book Belongs To: .................................................

.....................................................................................

.....................................................................................

.....................................................................................

# COLOR TEST PAGE

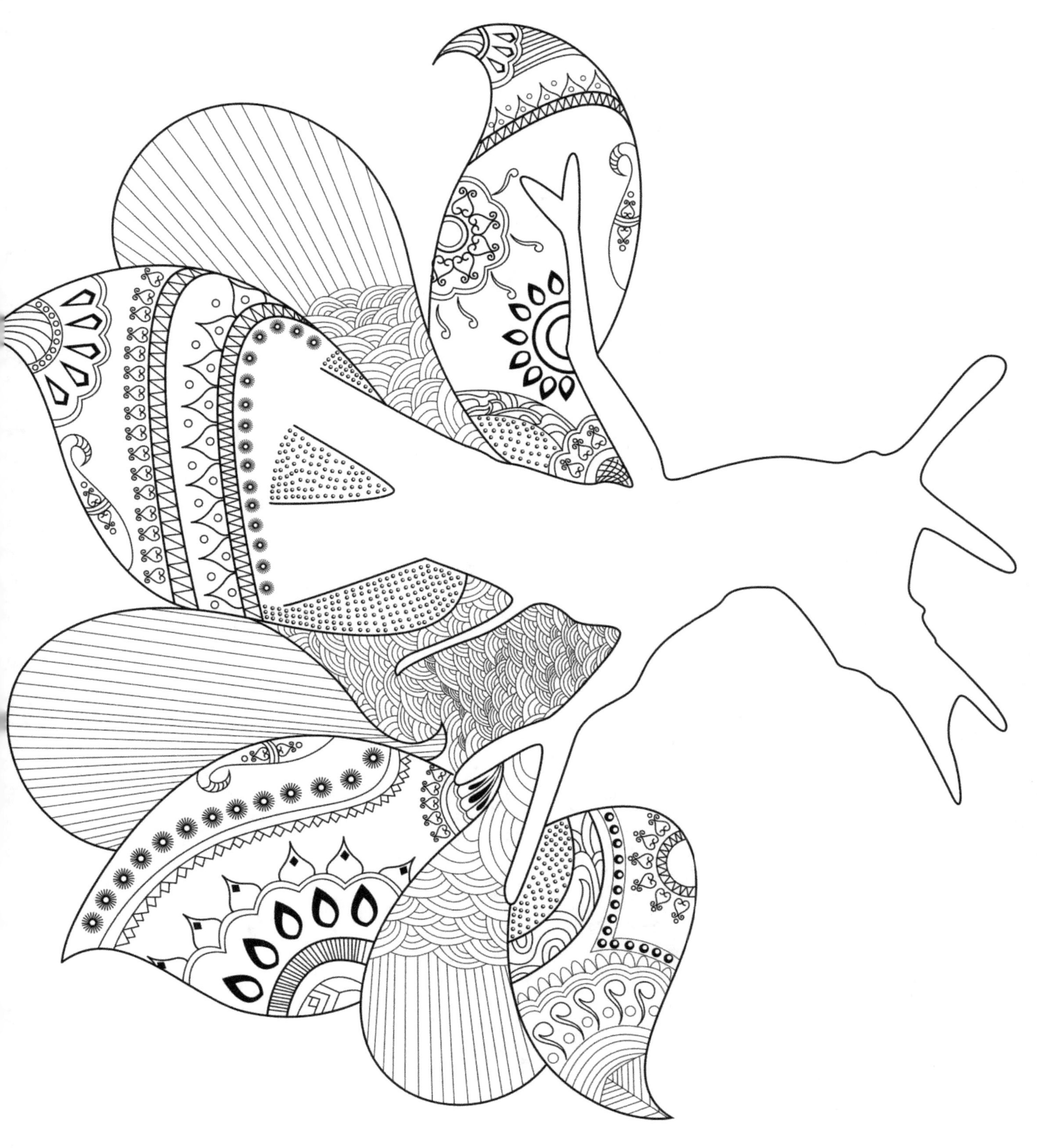

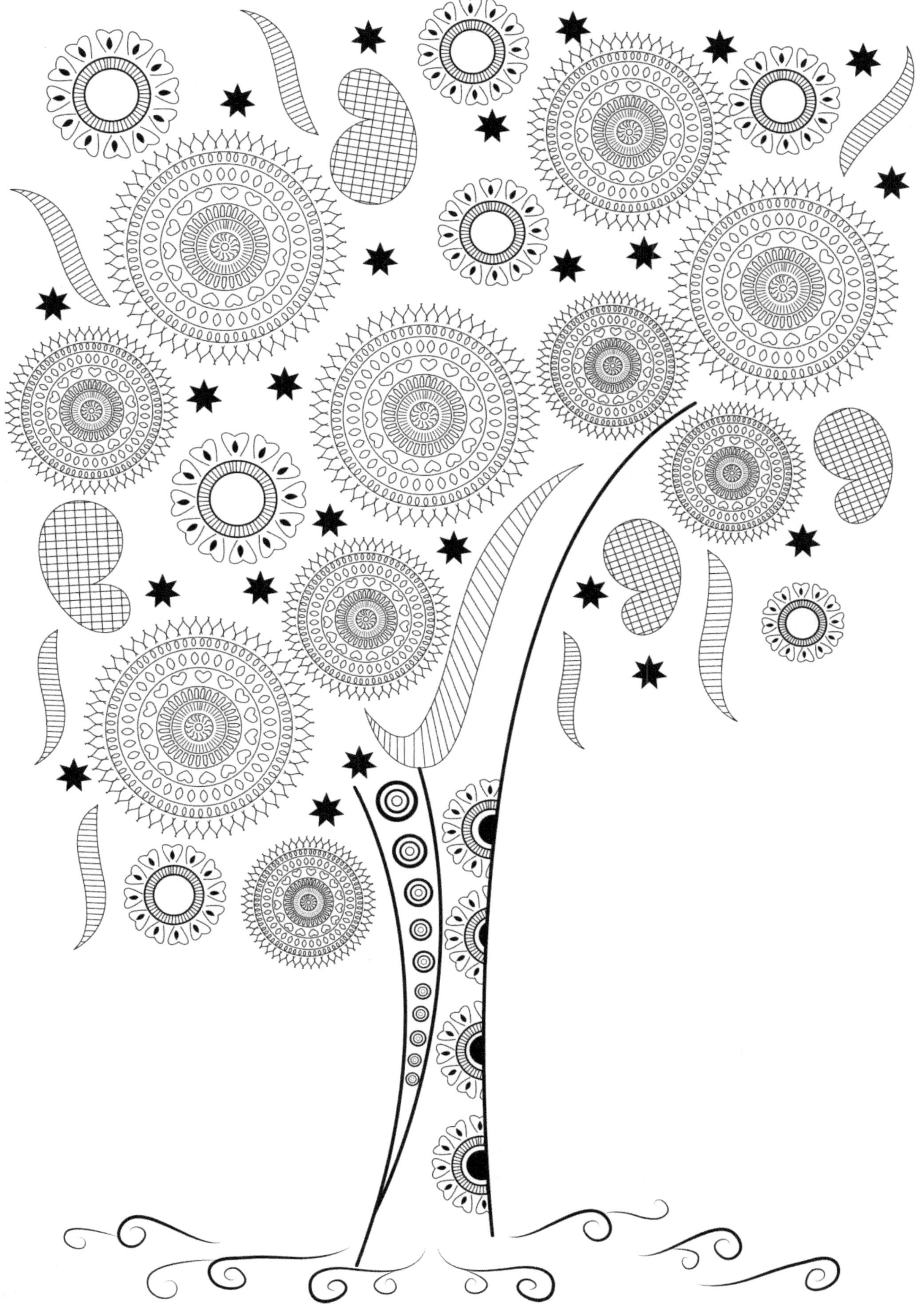

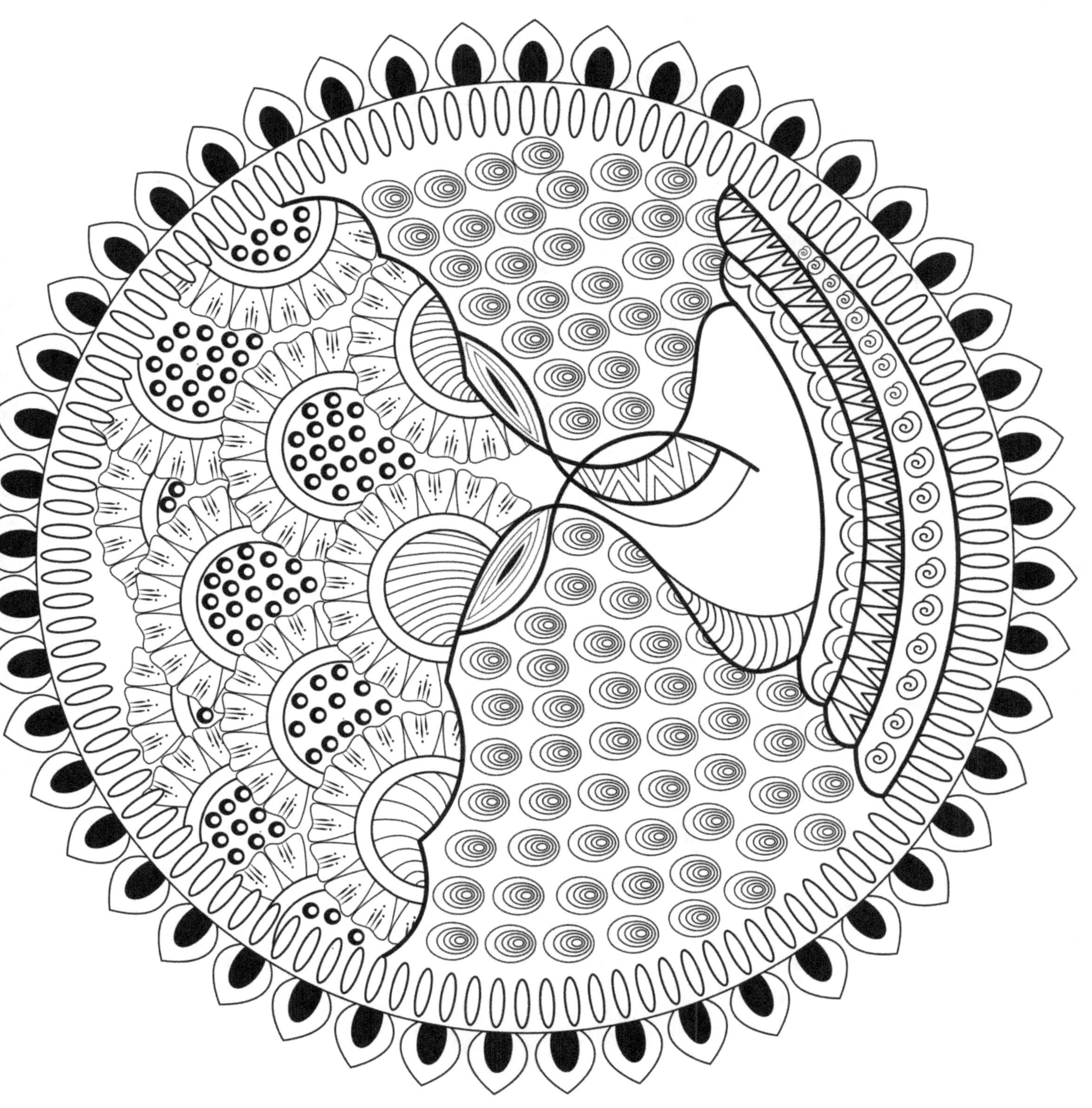

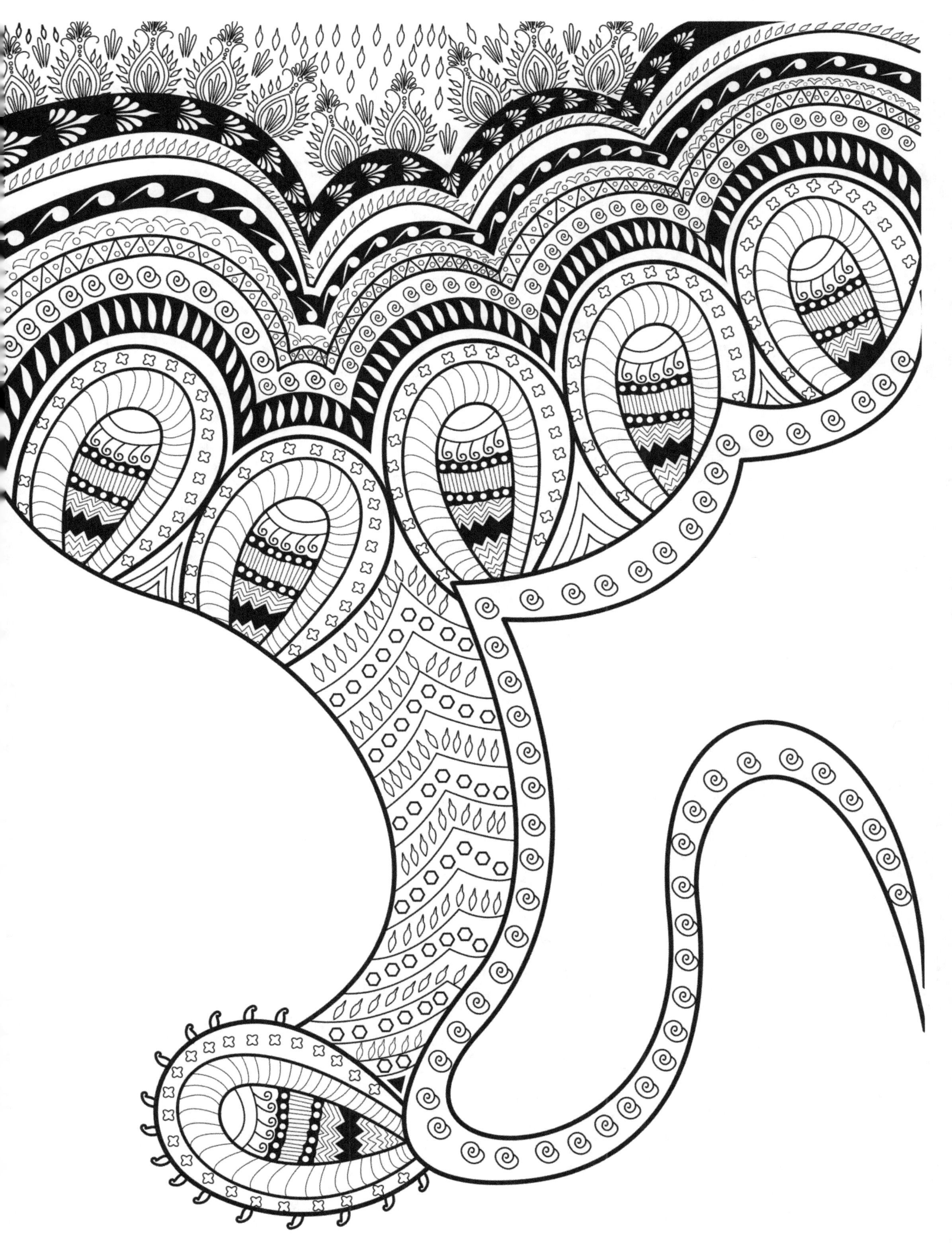

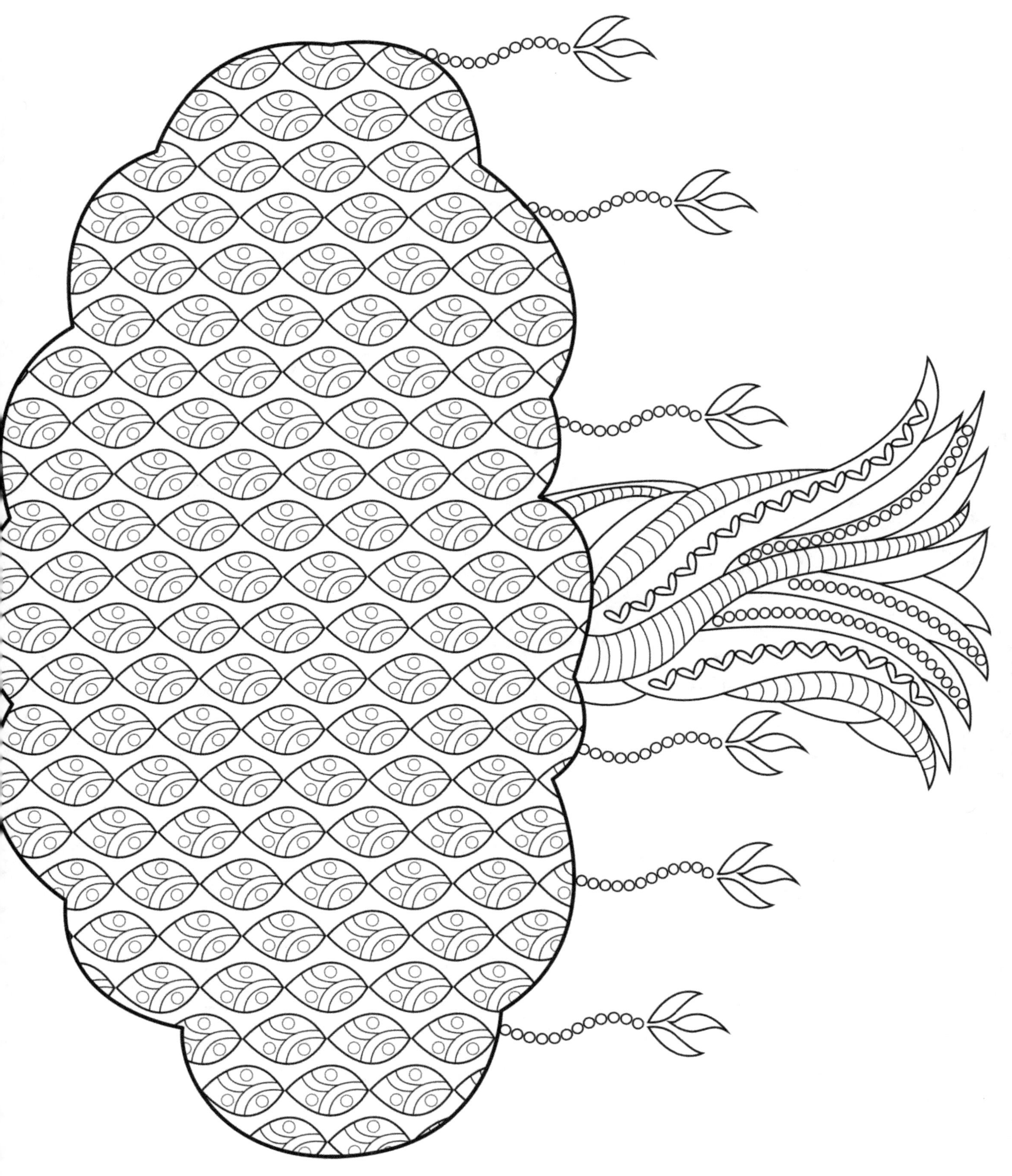

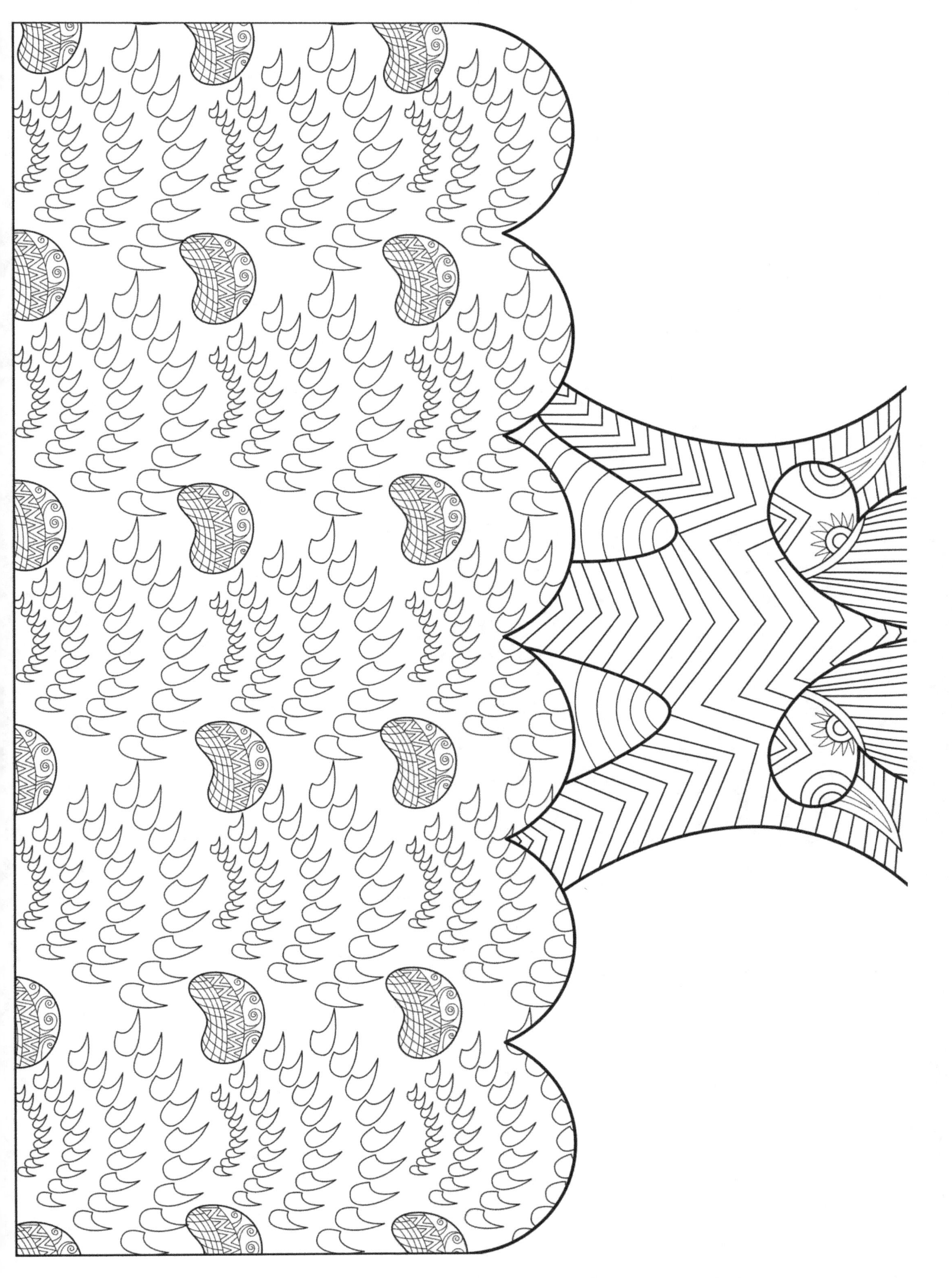

www.ingramcontent.com/pod-product-compliance
Lightning Source LLC
Chambersburg PA
CBHW081744250726
48657CB00010B/3406